A Kid's Guide to MYTHOLOGY

ZEUS

Don Nardo

Mitchell Lane
PUBLISHERS
P.O. Box 196
Hockessin, DE 19707
www.mitchelllane.com

Mitchell Lane
PUBLISHERS

Printing   1   2   3   4   5   6   7   8

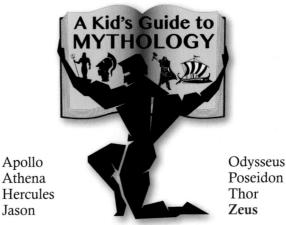

A Kid's Guide to
MYTHOLOGY

Apollo	Odysseus
Athena	Poseidon
Hercules	Thor
Jason	Zeus

Library of Congress Cataloging-in-Publication Data
Nardo, Don, 1947- author.
 Zeus / by Don Nardo.
    pages cm. — (A kid's guide to mythology)
 Summary: "Zeus is a figure in Greek mythology and the leader of the Olympians—the gods and goddesses who were worshiped by the ancient Greeks. The Greeks believed that Zeus and his followers defeated an earlier race of gods—the Titans—in a battle that burned the Earth's surface. Zeus established a home for himself and the other Olympian gods and goddesses above Mount Olympus, the tallest mountain in Greece. From that height, he kept a close eye on human affairs and when he felt it was necessary, he punished rule-breakers. Because he controlled thunder and lightning, punishment often took the form of his throwing a blazing thunderbolt at the offenders. In addition, Zeus pursued women—divine and human alike—and his wife (the goddess Hera) was often jealous. She used her powers to try to stop Zeus from fooling around. But he had many children with his mistresses, including the mighty hero Hercules."— Provided by publisher.
 Audience: Ages 8 to 11
 Audience: Grades 3 to 6
 Includes bibliographical references and index.
 ISBN 978-1-68020-004-1 (library bound)
 1. Zeus (Greek deity)—Juvenile literature. 2. Gods, Greek—Legends—Juvenile literature.
3. Mythology, Greek—Juvenile literature. I. Title.
 BL820.J8N37 2015
 292.2'113—dc23
                    2015017154

eBook ISBN: 978-1-68020-005-8

PUBLISHER'S NOTE: The Internet sites referenced herein were active as of the publication date. Due to the fleeting nature of some web sites, we cannot guarantee they will all be active when you are reading this book.

To reflect current usage, we have chosen to use the secular era designations BCE ("before the common era") and CE ("of the common era") instead of the traditional designations BC ("before Christ") and AD (anno Domini, "in the year of the Lord").

DISCLAIMER: Many versions of each myth exist today. The author is covering only one version of each story. Other versions may differ in details.

Contents

Words in **bold** throughout can be found in the Glossary.

This statue of Jupiter, the Roman version of Zeus, stands in modern Rome. It emphasizes Jupiter's role as bearer of justice by showing him grasping stone tablets containing laws.

1

THE DUDE WHO THREW THUNDERBOLTS

Zeus (ZOOS) is a name that many people today recognize. When someone asks, "Who was Zeus?" the answer is often something like, "Um, wasn't he the leader of the Greek gods?" Another common response is, "He's the dude who threw **thunderbolts** at people." It is not surprising that at least this much about him is fairly well known. After all, images from Greek mythology are widespread in modern books, graphic novels, TV shows, and movies.

Beyond that most people today know very little about Zeus. This is also not surprising. More than sixteen centuries have passed since the Greeks and Romans actually worshiped him. The Romans called him Jupiter (JU-puh-ter). In those days, almost everyone was very familiar with the many stories about his deeds and adventures.

Western Civilization's Founders
Today, those tales are called **myths** and only a few people know their details. Those who do take the time to learn about Zeus and his exploits are never disappointed. They

find that he was not only one of the most important gods in human history, but he was also an extremely colorful and entertaining character.

Historians are not exactly sure where and when Zeus originated. They do know that he was worshiped even before he became the Classical Greeks' main god. *Classical Greeks* is a term invented by modern scholars who use it to describe the residents of Greece from roughly the 700s to 300s BCE. That period ran from about twenty-seven hundred to twenty-three hundred years ago.

During those centuries, the Greeks accomplished a great deal in the arts, architecture, and literature. They built majestic temples dedicated to Zeus and other deities. Also, they invented democracy, philosophy, science, and the theater. As a result, people today see them as the founders of **Western civilization**. *Western* means Europe-centered and also refers to the places that Europeans colonized, including the United States.

More than a thousand years before the era of the Classical Greeks, people who spoke an early form of Greek entered Greece. **Archaeological** discoveries suggest that the early Greeks migrated from Anatolia (Turkey). It is uncertain why they migrated westward, but when they did, they brought with them an ancient god named Dyeus. It may have been pronounced something like dee-YOOS. And over time, the "d" sound changed into a "z" sound, making it Zeus.

Like other gods throughout history, Dyeus/Zeus possessed certain **attributes**. Modern language experts think the word *dyeus* originally meant sky. So the earliest version of Zeus was likely a deity of the sky and heavens. This would also explain why he became associated with thunder, thunderbolts (lightning), and storms. In fact, the thunderbolt became one of his **symbols**. The others were the eagle, the bull, and the oak tree.

Protector of Strangers

The Classical Greeks believed that Zeus also oversaw law, morality, and justice. These concepts were, and still are, related to protecting people. So the Greeks saw him as their divine protector. In that role, he was often called Zeus Polieus (poh-LY-us), which meant "Zeus of the city." To the Greeks of that time, a "city" was not just a big town. It was a *polis*, or **city-state**. Each city-state was a small nation consisting of a central town surrounded by villages and farmlands. There were hundreds of these small nations in and around the Greek mainland. No united country of Greece existed until the present one arose in the 1800s.

Each city-state had a **patron deity**, and that god favored that tiny nation and looked out for it. For example, Athena (uh-THEE-nuh), goddess of war and wisdom, was the patron goddess of Athens. And the patron god of the city-state of Corinth was Poseidon (puh-SY-din), who ruled the seas; however, because Zeus was the leader of the gods, he was in a sense the overall patron deity for all Greeks everywhere.

One of Zeus's other common names was Zeus Xenios (ZEE-nee-us). It translates as "Zeus the protector of strangers." This attribute reflected that he was in charge of **hospitality**—welcoming strangers and foreigners. People believed that he punished anyone who disrespected or abused a stranger.

Zeus and his fellow gods were also thought to have certain physical and emotional attributes. The Greeks

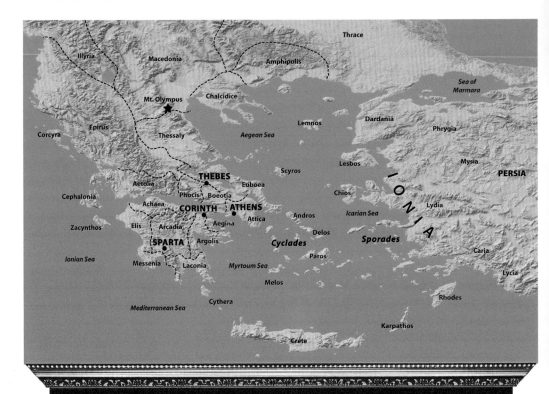

The following labels appear on the map: Thrace, Illyria, Macedonia, Amphipolis, Sea of Marmara, Mt. Olympus, Chalcidice, Corcyra, Epirus, Thessaly, Lemnos, Dardania, Phrygia, Mysia, Aegean Sea, Lesbos, PERSIA, Scyros, THEBES, Aetolia, Euboea, Chios, Cephalonia, Phocis, Boeotia, Lydia, Achaea, CORINTH, ATHENS, Andros, Icarian Sea, Zacynthos, Elis, Arcadia, Aegina, Attica, Delos, SPARTA, Argolis, Cyclades, Sporades, Caria, Ionian Sea, Messenia, Laconia, Myrtoum Sea, Paros, Lycia, Melos, Mediterranean Sea, Cythera, Rhodes, Karpathos, Crete, IONIA

This map shows some of the better-known ancient Greek city-states, whose residents all worshiped Zeus. The two militarily strongest city-states were Sparta, with the finest land army, and Athens, with the largest navy.

believed that the deities looked and acted like humans. Zeus and several other gods got married and had children. Some had children out of wedlock, too. They also lost their tempers, fought among themselves, and made mistakes, just like people. Clearly, picturing the gods this way made it easier for people to understand and pray to those divine beings.

Still, having human form and personalities did not make the gods exactly the same as people. Two critical factors separated the two races. First, the gods were much more powerful than people. In the words of the fifth-century BCE Greek poet Pindar, "Single is the race, single of men and gods. From a single mother we both draw breath. But a difference of power in everything keeps us apart."[1] Thus, the Greeks believed that the gods, especially their leader, Zeus, could instantly overpower or kill even the strongest human.

The second factor that made gods like Zeus different from people had to do with aging. As everyone knows, humans grow old and eventually die. In contrast, the Greek gods did *not* age. Instead, they were **immortal**, meaning they lived forever.

The Father of Gods and Men
The Greeks believed that being immortal and having superior powers and strength made the gods worthy of worship. Greek worship was based primarily on honoring and pleasing Zeus and his fellow deities. For example, carving statues of Zeus and building temples dedicated to him were ways of honoring him.

The most famous temple of Zeus was at Olympia, in southwestern Greece, erected between 470 and 454 BCE. The **renowned** athletic games named for that place—the Olympic games—were held in his honor. Inside Zeus's enormous temple rested the best known of the many statues of him. It was the work of Phidias (FID-ee-us) in 430 BCE, today seen as the ancient world's finest sculptor. He also created the famous statue of Athena that stood inside the Parthenon temple in Athens.

The statue of Zeus at Olympia was later recognized as one of the seven wonders of the ancient world. The ancient Greek geographer Strabo (STRAY-boh) saw it and wrote that it was "made of ivory." He added that Phidias "represented the god as seated," with the head almost touching "the peak of the roof." It therefore gave "the impression that, if Zeus were to stand up straight, he would take the roof off the temple!"[2]

Holding religious festivals at certain times of the year also honored Zeus. And the belief was that **sacrificing**, or making offerings to him, greatly pleased him. The offerings consisted of liquids, including wine, milk, and honey, and various plants. Also sacrificed were animals—pigs, goats, sheep, cattle, and birds. After the animals were killed their bodies were burned. It was thought that the smoke that rose up into the sky nourished Zeus. People also prayed to him and often asked him for favors.

Because of the central role that Zeus played in Greek religion and life, he appears in dozens of myths. One describes his birth and another his childhood. Still another tells how he defeated an earlier race of gods to become the leader of his own divine group, the **Olympians**. These tales appear in the *Theogony*, by the early Greek poet Hesiod (HES-ee-id). Several stories about Zeus tell about his romantic affairs with both goddesses and human women. And others involve the many children produced by those relationships. In addition, Zeus plays roles in a number of myths about battles and adventures. Hesiod called him "the father of gods and men." When he spoke, "all the gods, [and] givers of gifts, applauded him."[3] Today, thousands of years later, thanks to never-ending retellings of the myths, the chief Olympian is still respected and admired.

THE DOVES OF DODONA

One of the major ancient Greek shrines to Zeus was the **oracle** at Dodona in northwestern Greece. In the ancient world, an oracle was a priestess (or less often a priest) who supposedly conveyed messages from a god to humans. The place where she did this, and the messages themselves, were also called oracles. Zeus's shrine at Dodona was the second most famous oracle in the Greek world. The most famous oracle was that of Apollo (uh-PAHL-oh), god of **prophecy**, at Delphi in central Greece. (Prophecy was the act of foretelling future events.) People believed that Zeus gave advice and announced prophecies through the oracles that dwelled at Dodona. At first, they were priests called Selli. By the 400s BCE, however, the Dodona oracles were priestesses known as "Doves."

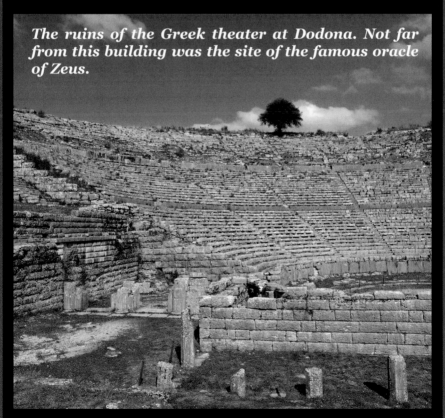

The ruins of the Greek theater at Dodona. Not far from this building was the site of the famous oracle of Zeus.

This early modern painting depicts Cronos, leader of the Titans, the first race of Greek gods.

Zeus and the
Olympian Gods

The earliest—and one of the more important—myths about Zeus tells about his origins. It describes how the world he inherited came to be, and it explains how he and his siblings fought a bloody war against the first race of gods—the **Titans** (TY-tnz).

Like Zeus, the Titans had human features. Unlike people, however, the Titans were gigantic. They were said to stand taller than a three-story house. The huge, powerful deities arrived on the scene not long after the universe itself emerged.

Before that epic event, the Greeks believed that Chaos was the only place that existed. Chaos was dark and filled with big, swirling masses of rocks, dust, air, and water. No one knows how long it existed. It might have been hundreds or even thousands of centuries.

Rise of the Titans

Then, as if out of nowhere, a series of strange beings sprang out of Chaos. The most important of their number was Eros (EE-rohs), the force of love. He gave off glowing light that shattered the darkness and he brought form and substance to the world. He made the heavier elements within Chaos sink down and become the earth, with its mountains and seas. Eros also caused the lighter parts inside Chaos to float upward and become the sky.

Next, Eros's love brought about a new miracle. The two regions—earth and sky—acquired the spark of life and personality. The earth became Gaia (GAY-uh), Mother Earth. And the sky became Uranus (YUR-uh-nis), Father Heaven. Gaia and Uranus soon mated and produced numerous children. Among them were twelve who had human shape. Making up the first race of gods, they became known as the Titans. They included Hyperion (hy-PEER-ee-in), the sun god; Thea (TAY-uh), goddess of the moon; and the most powerful of the lot—Cronos (KROH-nus).

Cronos was so strong that he managed to overthrow his father, Uranus, and take charge of the universe. Cronos also married another Titan, Rhea (REE-uh). And they began having children. The problem was that Cronos grew fearful that his children might attack him, as he had attacked Uranus. To remedy this situation, Cronos stood beside Rhea during each of her childbirths. When a baby appeared, he grabbed it and swallowed it whole. (Living inside his belly, these gods were still alive and continued to age. They were, after all, immortal.)

After seeing five of her children swallowed by her husband, Rhea decided she had had enough. When the time came to have her sixth child, Zeus, she snuck away from Cronos. And after the infant was born, she hid it in a cave on the large Greek island of Crete. Of course, she realized that her husband would demand that she give him the new child to swallow. In her favor, he was a bit dim-witted. So she tricked him. In Hesiod's words, she handed him "a giant stone." Eagerly, he "thrust it down into his belly, the fool! He did not know that his son, no stone, was left behind, unhurt and undefeated."[1]

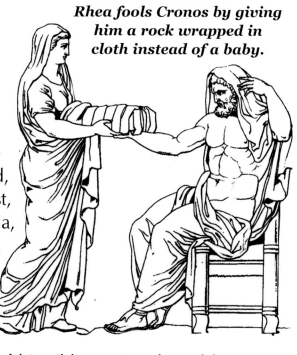

Rhea fools Cronos by giving him a rock wrapped in cloth instead of a baby.

To Control the Universe
In the years that followed, at Rhea's request, Zeus's grandmother, Gaia, secretly raised the child. He grew up extremely strong, handsome, and bright. One of the chief facts Gaia taught him was the grisly fate of his siblings. It sickened him to think that his brothers and sisters were still trapped inside Cronos's belly.

So when Zeus became a young adult, he decided to help his brothers and sisters. Gaia gave him some strong medicine that made anyone who took it throw up. And he sneaked a large dose of the stuff into Cronos's breakfast. It worked! The king of the Titans frowned, belched, and then started vomiting. First, he threw up the stone that Rhea had given him in place of Zeus. Then, one by one, out came the five children, now grown into adults. There was Demeter (dem-EE-ter), followed by Hades (HAY-deez), Hera (HEAR-uh), Hestia (HES-tee-uh), and Poseidon.

Cronos was both shaken by what had happened and afraid. And he had good reason to fear, because Zeus and his siblings now joined forces against their father. A tremendous war for control of the universe ensued. Most of the Titans naturally fought alongside their leader, Cronos. But a few of them abandoned their race and fought for Zeus. This was because they recognized that Zeus was smarter and more just than Cronos. Among the Titans who helped Zeus were the clever Prometheus (pro-MEE-thee-us) and his mentally slow but brave brother Epimetheus (ep-uh-MEE-thee-us).

During the war, Zeus frequently hurled thunderbolts at his enemies. Those frightening, white-hot weapons thereafter became one of his trademarks. Meanwhile, his brother, Hades, had the benefit of a special cap. When Hades put the cap on his head, he instantly became invisible. And that allowed him to sneak up unseen on an enemy. As for Poseidon, he fought mostly with a **trident**, a deadly three-pronged spear.

Zeus prepares to hurl one of his trademark thunderbolts.

Those and other weapons gave Zeus's side a small advantage in the war, but it was still a long, brutal struggle. Part of Hesiod's description of that awful conflict calls it a "hateful battle." As the two groups of gods clashed, "the boundless sea roared terribly around. The great earth rumbled and broad heaven groaned." Indeed, the ground shook so violently that Mt. Olympus, Greece's tallest peak "was disturbed down to its roots." The opposing warriors "hurled their wounding missiles, and the voices of both sides, shouting, reached the starry sky." For ten long years, massive fires scorched earth's shaking, **seething** surface. "To the eye," Hesiod added, "it looked as though broad heaven were coming down upon the earth."[2]

Commander and Father Figure

Finally, Zeus and his followers were victorious. They now proceeded to banish Cronos and most of the other Titans. The defeated giants were condemned to spend eternity in a dark, miserable underground realm called Tartarus. Prometheus, Epimetheus, and the other Titans who had aided Zeus fared better. They were allowed to stay and live on earth's surface.

After they won the war, Zeus and his divine followers took charge of the universe. Their main residence became the summit of towering Mt. Olympus. There, they erected a cluster of splendid palaces. Based on the mountain's name, they became known as the Olympian gods.

Because Zeus had led the rebellion against the Titans, it seemed only natural that he should be the leader of the Olympians. He was also far stronger than the other gods. His claim that he could win a tug of war against all the rest combined was only slightly exaggerated. So from then on, he ruled the Olympians. In the roles of commander and father figure, he became known for his wisdom. "I trust wise Zeus," Hesiod remarked, partly because he "sees all and understands."[3]

Of course, Hesiod was a human being. Moreover, at the time that Zeus first took control of the world, humans did not yet exist. Zeus, the king of Olympus, would soon play an important role in the creation of humans.

A modern statue of the sea god Poseidon shows him holding his famous trident.

ZEUS AND THE GIGANTOMACHY

The defeat of the Titans was not the only war that Zeus took part in against non-humans. He also fought a conflict against an army of ugly, human-shaped giants. Before Zeus's birth, his father Cronos had badly injured his own father Uranus in their struggle for control of the universe. The blood from Uranus's wounds had formed droplets and each droplet had rapidly grown into a giant. Although Zeus's grandmother, Gaia, had raised him, she later grew angry with him. It pained her that he had locked away her offspring, the Titans, in dark Tartarus. So she called on the giants to attack and overthrow Zeus. The Classical Greeks called this mighty battle the Gigantomachy (gee-gan-TOM-uh-kee), and they often depicted it in paintings, sculptures, and literature. Aided by several of the Olympian gods, Zeus eventually won the fight against the giants. Particularly valiant and helpful in the victory was Zeus's muscular, fearless son. Half-god and half-**mortal**, his name was Heracles (HAIR-uh-kleez). Later, the Romans called him Hercules (HER-kyoo-leez), the name by which he is best known today.

This carved stone panel, on display at Delphi (in central Greece), depicts the fierce battle known as the Gigantomachy.

This statue of the Titan Prometheus, created in 1762, now rests in the Louvre Museum in Paris, France.

3

ZEUS AND THE CREATURES OF PROMETHEUS

Not only did Zeus establish the Olympian gods, he also ordered the creation of human beings to populate the earth. Several versions of this human creation myth existed in ancient times. In the most popular one, the Titan Prometheus, aided by his brother Epimetheus, carried out the chief god's order. Prometheus soon did something behind Zeus's back, however, and this angered Zeus so much that he inflicted a terrible punishment on the Titan. The ancient Greeks viewed this quarrel between Zeus and Prometheus as one of the greatest stories ever told.

Naked and Shoeless

That tale begins a few years after Zeus had defeated the Titans, with the aid of Prometheus and Epimetheus. All the immortals admired Prometheus, in part because he was extremely wise and observant. In fact, those abilities earned him the job of Zeus's leading advisor.

One day, Zeus summoned Prometheus and told him he had an important task for him—to create animals and a race of humans to dwell on the earth. Prometheus was to be in charge of the project, Zeus said, but he could enlist the help of his brother, Epimetheus, if he so desired.

Excited by this assignment, Prometheus got right to work. According to the Roman myth-teller Ovid (AH-vid), he "took the new-made earth" and mixed it with rainwater, and then Prometheus "fashioned it into the image of the all-governing gods." The clever Titan also created all of the different kinds of animals. But, while "other animals hang their heads and look at the ground, he made man stand erect, bidding him look up to heaven and lift his head to the stars."[1]

Having taken this first step, Prometheus asked his brother to give the animals and humans various traits and abilities. The well-meaning Epimetheus did so, but because he was a bit scatter-brained, he failed to think things through before he acted. Epimetheus gave most of the best physical features to the animals. These included strength, swiftness, protective shells, and wings to achieve flight; also, some animals he clothed "with thick skins sufficient to defend against the winter cold," as the Greek scholar Plato (PLAY-toh) told it.[2] Epimetheus used up most of the physical gifts on the animals, so humans were left with very little to help them prosper and survive.

Prometheus immediately noticed the problem when he inspected his brother's work. It was obvious that the humans were "naked and shoeless," Plato wrote. They "had neither beds nor weapons of defense."[3]

Plato

22

Upset, Prometheus wondered what he could do to reverse Epimetheus's terrible blunder.

Then Prometheus had one of his numerous clever ideas. He saw that his newly made human creatures would be able to survive if they had the advantage of fire and its many uses. With it, they could cook raw food and make metals for tools and weapons. They could also provide heat for cold winter nights. Prometheus explained all this to Zeus and asked if he could provide the humans with the knowledge of fire, but the leader of the gods said no. Humans were unworthy of receiving the divine flicker of fire.

The Sting of Divine Wrath

Prometheus was surprised by and disappointed in Zeus's decision. The Titan was so troubled that he decided to disobey his divine master. Prometheus went to the workshop where Hephaestus (heh-FES-tis), god of the forge, often worked. There, after Hephaestus had left to do an errand, Prometheus swiped a bit of fire and hid it in a hollow reed. Hurrying to a group of humans, Prometheus gave them the fire and taught them how to preserve it. He also instructed them in the many ways to use that sometimes dangerous, precious resource.

It did not take long for Zeus to discover what Prometheus had done. The ruler of Olympus was furious that his trusted assistant had deceived him. First, Prometheus must be punished, Zeus decided, and then the humans, too, would feel the sting of divine **wrath**.

Zeus wasted no time in ordering two gods to bring the disobedient Titan to him. Then, in Hesiod's words, "Clever Prometheus was bound by Zeus in cruel

A 1637 oil painting portrays Prometheus carrying some fire from heaven to give to his beloved creations —human beings.

chains, unbreakable, chained round a pillar." Then Zeus summoned and "set on him an eagle with long wings, which came and ate his liver each night."[4] Because Prometheus was immortal, however, his liver grew back during the daytime. As a result, just as Zeus intended, the chained deity was forced to endure hours of horrible pain each and every night.

After that, whenever anyone walked by and asked why Prometheus was chained, he was not shy about telling them. "See me, a miserable prisoner!" he cried out, according to the fifth-century BCE Athenian playwright Aeschylus (ES-kuh-lis). The Titan claimed to be the sad "enemy of Zeus," who all the gods now distrust "because I was too good a friend to men!"[5]

Once he had punished Prometheus, the still-angry Zeus turned to humanity. There were several penalties that Zeus laid on the earliest men and women. In one, he decided to send a massive flood to drown and destroy what Zeus called the vile "creatures of Prometheus."

It was fortunate for the humans that Prometheus learned about the plan. Although he was a prisoner, he was able to warn his son Deucalion (du-KAL-yin). Shortly before the flood came, Deucalion

A bust of the Athenian playwright Aeschylus.

A stone sculpture shows Deucalion and his wife, Pyrrha, selecting stones that will become more people.

and his wife Pyrrha (PEER-ra) climbed to the summit of a tall mountain. There, they were safe and managed to survive the disaster, which wiped out the rest of humankind.

After the flood was over, the couple gathered hundreds of little stones, and as they walked along, they tossed out the stones. The stones soon grew into human beings, who got together and created even more human beings. In this way, Zeus's plan, conceived in anger, backfired on him, and he learned that he, just like the humans he ruled over, was far from perfect.

THE IMPORTANCE OF HOSPITALITY

The Classical Greeks had a second myth in which Zeus sent a flood to kill humans. It was connected to that god's role as overseer of hospitality—the welcoming of strangers. One day Zeus desired to find out if the residents of a certain Greek region treated outsiders with respect, so he summoned the messenger god, Hermes (HER-meez), and the two dressed like poor beggars. After they arrived they began going from house to house, both rich and poor. In each case, they politely begged for a bit of food and a place to sleep. Zeus was soon sorely disappointed. In stop after stop, he found the local people both rude and cruel. The owners of a thousand houses in a row told him and his companion to go away. Finally, the two deities came to the smallest and poorest hut in the entire region. The owners were an elderly couple, Baucis (BAW-kis) and Philemon (FIL-uh-mon). They welcomed the visitors and did everything they could to make them comfortable. Much impressed, Zeus revealed himself to the old couple. He and Hermes took them to a nearby mountaintop, and there, Baucis and Philemon watched as Zeus punished their neighbors by drowning the whole region beneath a large flood. When the waters had **receded**, Zeus turned the couple's hut into a splendid mansion. And years later, when they died, he changed them into trees whose trunks were joined together as one for all eternity.

Hermes

Even though she was Zeus's sister, Demeter, pictured here, was one of his many romantic partners.

4

ZEUS'S ROVING EYE AND HERA'S JEALOUSY

When Zeus was not fighting his enemies and punishing wrongdoers, he tried to enjoy himself in his free time. It turned out that his favorite pastime was romancing members of the fairer sex. If he lived in modern society, people would call him a "ladies' man." Sometimes his love interests were goddesses. Other times they were mortal women. Also, in some cases he married them, while in others he cheated behind their backs. Over time, those relationships resulted in the production of many dozens of offspring, and several of those children became famous characters in Greek mythology.

Gods Have Their Own Laws

After he defeated the Titans and became ruler of the Olympian gods, Zeus took his first **consort**, or wife. She was Metis (MEE-tis), a daughter of two of the Titans who had sided with him in the war. In fact, an entire new generation of Titans was born of Zeus's Titan allies. Metis was not only beautiful, but she was also smart and thoughtful. So she came to be known as a goddess of wisdom. According to Hesiod, "Zeus, king of the gods, first took to wife Metis, wisest of all the gods and men."[1]

Zeus and Metis were happy for a while, but the fact that she was smarter than he was bothered him, so he got rid of her by swallowing her. At the time, he did not realize she was pregnant, and the result was that their daughter was born by bursting out of Zeus's head. That daughter, the famous Athena, came out fully-grown. Because her mother was quite intelligent, she too became a goddess of wisdom. Athena was dressed in full armor and held a spear and shield, so she became the Olympian goddess of war.

Zeus was unable to go very long without female companionship. Not long after Athena's birth, he took a second consort, another young Titan whose name was Themis (THEE-mis). She bore Zeus the Hours (the three Seasons—Spring, Summer, and Winter), who caused the stars to migrate across the heavens from month to month. The divine couple also produced the Fates: Clotho/CLO-thoh (the Spinner), Lachesis/La-CHEE-sis (the drawing of lots), and Atropos/A-TRO-pos (inevitable—not to be avoided). Those three goddesses had the task of assigning humans their individual destinies.

As happened to him often, Zeus soon grew tired of Themis, and he began a relationship with a nature goddess, or **nymph**, named Eurynome (YUR-in-uh-mee). That affair was still going on when he started seeing his own sister. Today, people frown on romances between brothers and sisters, but this social **taboo** did not exist for the Greek Olympian gods. As Ovid put it, "Gods have married their sisters!" Why? "The gods have their own laws. What is the use of trying to relate human conduct to the ways of heaven, when they are governed by different rules?"[2]

The divine sister in this case was Demeter, goddess of plants and agriculture. "Demeter, who feeds all," Hesiod wrote, "came to the bed of Zeus."[3] The product of that union was an attractive, fun-loving young woman named Persephone (per-SEF-uh-nee) who eventually wedded Zeus's brother, Hades, ruler of the Underworld. This came about because Zeus and Hades worked out a scheme that enabled Hades, the lord of the dark realm, to kidnap Persephone.

Queen of the Gods

Zeus's romantic affairs continued as he hooked up with two more young Titans—Mnemosyne (nem-OZ-in-ee) and Leto (LEE-toh). Leto bore him two of his most famous and important children, the twin Olympian deities Apollo and Artemis (AR-tuh-mis). The **versatile** Apollo oversaw prophecy, healing, poetry, archery, and music. And Artemis was in charge of hunting and a defender of all wild animals.

Zeus's most famous consort came directly after Leto. Often depicted in myths as the official queen of the Olympian gods, she was Hera, another of Zeus's sisters. Zeus and Hera had an especially colorful first meeting. He saw her in a meadow one winter day and tricked her by turning himself into a cuckoo bird. As that creature, he pretended to be freezing to death. And taking pity on the poor bird, she held it to her chest to keep it warm. Zeus then turned back into his normal form, so that the two deities were then in a tight embrace. Their relationship developed from there.

Almost from the beginning, Hera was jealous of her new husband's love affairs. Even though Zeus and Leto had already parted ways, Leto was pregnant with Apollo and Artemis—and Hera did her best to make trouble for Leto. Hera forbade people almost everywhere from giving the pregnant goddess shelter. Only after Zeus himself stepped in did Leto give birth to the twins on the tiny Greek island of Delos.

Even more spiteful was Hera's treatment of Semele (SEM-uh-lee), a princess of the Greek city of Thebes. The trouble began when Hera found out that her husband had made the young woman pregnant.

Shaking with anger, Hera came up with an unusually cruel punishment. Hera tricked Zeus into showing Semele his true form, which only gods could see without dying. That form was so bright that it burned the girl to ashes.

At the last moment Zeus managed to save the baby from Semele's womb before it, too, was destroyed. That fortunate infant was Dionysus (dy-uh-NY-sus). He became the fun-loving god of the grape and wine.

And so it went. Zeus's eye constantly roved to other women and Hera was always upset by it. At one point, according to the Greek poet Homer (HO-mer), Zeus urged Hera to stop being so jealous. She watched his every move, he complained. "But you shall gain nothing by it," he warned. "You will only make me dislike you." And things "will only be more unpleasant for you."[4] Zeus was wasting his breath, of course. Wherever the Greek gods dwell today, Hera remains as jealous as ever.

ZEUS AND EUROPA

One of Zeus's most fun-filled romantic affairs was with a young woman named Europa (yur-OH-puh). He saw her playing with some girlfriends at a beach in what is now Lebanon. Strongly drawn to her, he played a trick by changing himself into a bull, and then he strode along the beach until he reached the girls. They saw that the bull was beautiful and they petted it like most people pet a dog or cat. To Zeus's delight, Europa decided to jump on the bull's back and ride it. When she was securely in place atop the creature, it suddenly ran into the sea and began swimming. As Europa held on for dear life, the bull swam hundreds of miles, ending up in Crete. There, Zeus revealed himself as a god, but in a form that was safe for the girl to look at. Europa and Zeus became lovers and she bore him Minos, who later became a famous Cretan king. Centuries later some Greeks named the continent of Europe after her.

Europa and Zeus

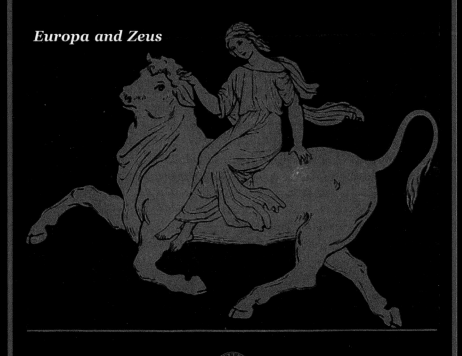

Dating from the first century CE (about nineteen centuries ago), this is a Roman copy of the Greek sculptor Phidias's statue of Zeus at Olympia.

5

Zeus's Firm Place in Popular Culture

Zeus ended up having a comfortable and secure place in popular culture, which includes familiar ideas, images, and characters, past and present, that most Americans, British, and other Westerners share. In Europe and elsewhere, Zeus's place in popular culture went through two phases. One occurred in ancient times and the other in modern times.

In the ancient phase, Zeus became a permanent part of popular culture as people erected shrines dedicated to him. One of those shrines was the famous temple and statue at Olympia. True wonders of the world, they stood there even after Rome conquered the Greek lands in the century or so following 200 BCE. Rome preserved Greek temples, along with statues of Zeus and other gods, because the Romans admired Greece's culture and they often borrowed ideas from it that they liked.

Choosing the Moral Option
A good example involved religious ideas and images. Jupiter, the head god of Rome's official state religion, was mostly based on Zeus. The Romans even retained and

retold the Greek myths about Zeus. They simply changed Zeus's name to Jupiter in those tales. Similarly, the Romans changed the name of Zeus's wife, Hera, to Juno (JU-noh).

Zeus/Jupiter's temples and statues remained in place for a long a time. Only when Christianity became Rome's official religion in the late 300s CE did the situation start to change. Most Christians viewed Zeus and the other Olympians as false gods, so they defaced many of the statues and allowed the temples to decay. This process speeded up after Rome's fall in the late 400s CE. After that, Christianity completely replaced most of Europe's old faiths and the majority of Zeus's temples and their contents disappeared over time.

Another aspect of Zeus's place in ancient popular culture was his inclusion in plays. An outstanding example was Aeschylus's great play *Prometheus Bound*. It was written about 463 BCE and every Greek and Roman was familiar with the myth of Prometheus's crime of stealing fire from heaven and how Zeus punished him.

The ancient Greeks who watched Aeschylus's stirring story unfold on stage were reminded of their own lives. Many of them pictured themselves in Prometheus's place. He faced a difficult choice; he could either obey Zeus—the immoral option—or he could disobey him—the moral choice. The playgoers hoped that if they were in a similar situation, they would do as Prometheus did and they would have the courage to choose the moral option to help humans, even if they had to pay a penalty for it.

The Arts, Literature, and Movies

As the modern historian C.M. Bowra said, this drive to do the right thing whenever possible was strong among the ancient Greeks. It was not based on the hope of receiving a reward later in heaven; instead the Greeks' "own natures impelled them to do it." To be moral and good simply because honor demanded it was "long a feature of Greek thought." They "believed in their own human nature." So they "developed a morality which was founded on human values." Both Aeschylus and his audiences recognized those values.

In this scene from a modern production of Prometheus Bound, *the disobedient Titan is chained to a big rock in the foreground.*

That same myth, along with many others involving the Greco-Roman gods, survived after Rome's fall. During the medieval era, which began in the 500s and lasted until the 1500s, Europe's writers were Christians, yet they often mentioned the old mythical characters in their works.

Those mythical characters, including Zeus, became the subjects of painters. That was especially true during the Renaissance, the great flowering of the arts lasting from about 1300 to about 1550. In 1515 the noted Italian artist Dosso Dossi created a large oil painting that shows Zeus as an artist painting butterflies.

Through literature and art Zeus passed from ancient to medieval times and then to the early modern era. Modern painters and sculptors have frequently depicted Zeus and his colorful exploits. Frenchman Jean Ingres's 1811 work *Thetis Appeals to Zeus* shows the mighty god sitting on his throne atop Mt. Olympus. The sea nymph Thetis (THEE-tis) kneels before him, begging for a favor.

In the twentieth century and beyond, Zeus has remained a familiar figure in art and other areas of popular culture. One example is the video game *Zeus: Master of Olympus* by Vivendi Universal. It is set in the world of the mythical Greek gods. According to one online reviewer, "I can talk about everything I love about this game. But one thing absolutely fascinated me." Players can build a city almost from scratch, he says. Soon, "invaders start attacking your city." After a player asks Zeus for protection, that god destroys the invaders "by himself, even if you have no military. To me, this is one of the best city building games of all time!"[2]

Zeus has also been a frequent character in movies with mythical themes. The late, great actor Laurence Olivier played him in the 1981 film *Clash of the Titans*. In the 2010 movie remake, Liam Neeson played Zeus. Perhaps the most memorable onscreen Zeus was English actor Niall MacGinnis, in *Jason and the Argonauts* (1963). MacGinnis,

Italian artist Dosso Dossi's painting of Zeus, who is himself painting butterflies while the god Hermes (with the winged hat) urges others to be quiet.

alongside Honor Blackman as Hera, are wonderfully pictured as towering giants. The hero of the story, Jason, is only the size of a playing piece on Zeus's chessboard. Zeus will surely continue to entertain people for as long as people still find the Greek gods fascinating and fun.

Laurence Olivier, often called the greatest actor of the twentieth century, as he appeared as Zeus in Clash of the Titans *(1981).*

George Washington as Zeus?

In 1832, the US Congress wanted to honor the memory of the country's first president, George Washington, so the congressmen asked noted sculptor Horatio Greenough to create a statue of Washington. It was to be displayed inside the US Capitol building. Greenough based the work on ancient descriptions of Phidias's huge statue of Zeus at Olympia so he created the sculpture showing Washington sitting bare-chested on a throne in the same manner as the Olympian Zeus. When the work was completed in 1841 the sculptor was in for a surprise. Many Americans felt that showing Washington shirtless was offensive. Others thought the statue was funny. One critic declared, "It is a ridiculous affair. And instead of demanding admiration, it excites only laughter."[3] Someone else called the statue a "marble absurdity."[4] Because of this attitude, Congress moved Greenough's sculpture to the Capitol's east lawn in 1843. It moved again in 1908 to the Smithsonian Museum, and still again in 1964 to the National Museum of American History and Technology (now the National Museum of American History). Today, almost everyone who sees it agrees it is a masterpiece.

Horatio Greenough's splendid statue of George Washington posed as the Olympian Zeus now rests in the National Museum of American History, in Washington, DC.

CHAPTER NOTES

Chapter 1: The Dude Who Threw Thunderbolts

1. Pindar, *Odes*. In *Pindar: The Odes*. Trans. C.M. Bowra (New York: Penguin, 1985), 206.

2. J.J. Pollitt, ed. and trans. *The Art of Ancient Greece: Sources and Documents* (New York: Cambridge University Press, 1990), 61–62.

3. Hesiod, *Theogony*. In *Hesiod and Theognis*. Trans. Dorothea Wender (New York: Penguin, 1973), 44.

Chapter 2: Zeus and the Olympian Gods

1. Hesiod, *Theogony*, 39.

2. Ibid, 45–46.

3. Ibid, 67.

Chapter 3: Zeus and the Creatures of Prometheus

1. Ovid, *Metamorphoses*, trans. Mary M. Innes (London: Penguin, 1955), 31.

2. Plato, *Protagoras*. In *Plato, Dialogues*. Trans. Benjamin Jowett (Chicago: Encyclopedia Britannica, 1952), 44.

3. Ibid, 44.

4. Hesiod, *Theogony*, 40.

5. Aeschylus, *Prometheus Bound*. In *Aeschylus, Prometheus Bound, The Suppliants, Seven Against Thebes, The Persians*. Trans. Philip Vellacott (Baltimore: Penguin, 1961), 24.

Chapter 4: Zeus's Roving Eye and Hera's Jealousy

1. Hesiod, *Theogony*, 52.

2. Ovid, *Metamorphoses*, 216.

3. Hesiod, *Theogony*, 53.

4. Homer, *Iliad*. Trans. W.H.D. Rouse (New York: Signet, 1999), 21.

Chapter 5: Zeus's Firm Place in Popular Culture

1. C.M. Bowra. *The Greek Experience* (New York: Barnes and Noble, 1996), 67.

2. Derry Sexton, "Mythology Enthusiast Loves this Game!" http://www.amazon.com/Zeus-Master-Olympus-PC/product-reviews/B00004TJ2N/ref=cm_cr_pr_btm_link_3?ie=UTF8&pageNumber=3&showViewpoints=0&sortBy=bySubmissionDateDescending

3. U.S. Capitol Historical Society, "Washington on Display." https://uschs.wordpress.com/tag/george-washington-statue/

4. Ibid.

Works Consulted

Aeschylus, *Prometheus Bound*. In *Aeschylus, Prometheus Bound, The Suppliants, Seven Against Thebes, The Persians*. Trans. Philip Vellacott. Baltimore: Penguin, 1961.

Bellingham, David. *An Introduction to Greek Mythology*. Secaucus, NJ: Chartwell Books, 1989.

Bowra, C.M. *Classical Greece*. New York: Time-Life, 1977.

Bowra, C.M. *The Greek Experience*. New York: Barnes and Noble, 1996.

Burkert, Walter. *Greek Religion, Archaic and Classical*. Oxford, England: Basil Blackwell, 1985.

Grant, Michael. *A Guide to the Ancient World*. New York: Barnes and Noble, 1997.

Grant, Michael. *The Myths of the Greeks and Romans*. New York: Plume, 1995.

Grant, Michael and John Hazel. *Who's Who in Classical Mythology*. London: Routledge, 2002.

Hamilton, Edith. *Mythology*. New York: Grand Central, 1999.

Hesiod. *Theogony*. In *Hesiod and Theognis*. Trans. Dorothea Wender. New York: Penguin, 1973.

Howatson, M.C. and Ian Chilvers, eds. *The Concise Oxford Companion to Classical Literature*. New York: Oxford University Press, 2007.

Levi, Peter. *The Penguin History of Greek Literature*. New York: Penguin, 1987.

Martin, Thomas R. *Ancient Greece: From Prehistoric to Hellenistic Times*. New Haven: Yale University Press, 2000.

Matyszak, Philip. *The Greek and Roman Myths: A Guide to the Classical Stories*. London: Thames and Hudson, 2010.

Morford, Mark P.O. and Robert J. Lenardon, *Classical Mythology*. New York: Oxford University Press, 2010.

O'Sullivan, Maureen. *Greek Gods: An Iconoclast's Guide*. Athens: Efstathiadis Group, 1985.

Ovid. *Metamorphoses*. Trans. Mary M. Innes. London: Penguin, 1955.

Pindar. *The Odes*. Trans. C. M. Bowra. New York: Penguin, 1985.

Rouse, W.H.D. *Gods, Heroes and Men of Ancient Greece*. New York: New American Library, 2001.

Solomon, Jon. *The Ancient World in the Cinema*. New Haven: Yale University Press, 2001.

Stapleton, Michael. *The Illustrated Dictionary of Greek and Roman Mythology*. New York: Peter Bedrick, 1986.

FURTHER READING

Bingham, Jane M. *Ancient Greeks*. Hove, UK: Wayland, 2015.

Colavito, Jason. *Jason and the Argonauts Through the Ages*. Jefferson, NC: McFarland, 2014.

Evslin, Bernard. *Gods, Demigods, and Demons: The Encyclopedia of Greek Mythology*. New York: Open Road, 2012.

Ford, Michael. *Heroes, Gods, and Monsters of Ancient Greek Mythology*. Brighton, UK: Salariya, 2012.

Holm, Kirsten. *Everyday Life in Ancient Greece*. New York: Powerkids Press, 2012.

Houle, Muchelle M. *Gods and Goddesses in Greek Mythology Rock!* Berkely Heights, NJ: Enslow, 2011.

MacDonald, Fiona. *I Wonder Why the Greeks Built Temples*. New York: Kingfisher, 2012.

O'Connor, George. *Zeus: King of the Gods*. New York: First Second, 2010.

Rodgers, Nigel. *Everyday Life in Ancient Greece*. London: Hermes House, 2010.

Usborne. *Illustrated Stories from the Greek Myths*. London: Usborne, 2011.

Warner, Rex. *Men and Gods*. New York: NYRB, 2008.

On the Internet

The Creation of Man by Prometheus
    http://www.desy.de/gna/interpedia/greek_myth/creationMan.html
Encyclopedia Mythica: Zeus
    http://www.pantheon.org/articles/z/zeus.html
Greek Mythology for Kids
    http://greece.mrdonn.org/myths.html
Greek Mythology Link: Hera
    http://www.maicar.com/GML/Hera.html
Mythography: Zeus and Europa in Greek Mythology
    http://www.mythography.com/myth/welcome-to-mythography/
    greek-legends/lovers-2/zeus-europa
The Olympians
    http://www.desy.de/gna/interpedia/greek_myth/olympian.
    html#Olympians
Theoi Greek Mythology: Kronos (Cronos)
    http://www.theoi.com/Titan/TitanKronos.html
Theoi Greek Mythology: Zeus
    http://www.theoi.com/Olympios/Zeus.html
The Titans
    http://www.theoi.com/greek-mythology/titans.html
What are Myths?
    http://www.livingmyths.com/What.htm
Zeus and Prometheus: The Gift of Fire
    http://greece.mrdonn.org/greekgods/prometheus.html

GLOSSARY

archaeological (AR-kee-o-loj-i-cal)—the scientific study and examination of past peoples and cultures and what remains of the objects they used (architecture, art, tools, etc.)

attributes (AT-rih-byoots)—a god's personal traits, qualities, or powers

city-state (SI-tee state)—in ancient Greece, a small nation consisting of a central town and a number of outlying villages and farms

consort (KON-sort)—a spouse (husband or wife) or companion

hospitality (hah-spi-TAL-uh-tee)—the welcoming of strangers and foreigners

immortal (im-MOR-tl)—able to live forever

mortal (MOR-tl)—a human being

myths (miths)—stories about gods, heroes, monsters, and strange creatures relating to various religious beliefs of the past

nymph (nimf)—one of several groups of minor nature goddesses

Olympians (oh-LIM-pee-ins)—the group of gods led by Zeus and thought to live on top of Mt. Olympia, Greece's highest mountain

oracle (OR-uh-kl)—in the ancient world, a person, usually a priestess, thought to be a medium between the gods and humans; or the building in which an oracle conveyed a divine message; or the message itself

patron deity (PAY-trin DEE-uh-tee)—in the ancient world, a god or goddess who watched over and protected a specific city and its inhabitants

polis (POH-lis)—the Greek word for a city-state

prophecy (PRAH-fuh-see)—a prediction about future events

recede (ree-SEED)—to move back or away

renowned (ree-NOUN)—famous

sacrifice (SAK-ruh-fice)—an offering made to pacify or calm a god or goddess

seething (SEETH-ing)—angry

symbol (SIM-bl)—something that stands for or represents something else

taboo (ta-BOO)—forbidden, or frowned on

thunderbolt (THUN-der-bolt)—a bolt of lightning, which became one of Zeus's symbols

Titans (TY-tnz)—a race of gods that ruled the universe before the rise of the Olympians

trident (TRY-dnt)—a three-pronged spear; it was one of the sea god Poseidon's symbols

versatile (VER-suh-tl)—multi-talented

Western civilization (WEST-ern siv-a-le-ZAY-shen)—the culture or society that developed over time in Europe and the places colonized by Europeans around the world, including the United States, Australia, and New Zealand

wrath (RATH)—anger

INDEX

ABOUT THE AUTHOR

Historian and award-winning writer Don Nardo has published more than four hundred books for teens and children, along with a number of volumes for college and general adult readers. His specialty is the ancient world, including the histories, cultures, and myths of the Greeks, Romans, and peoples of Mesopotamia. Nardo also composes and arranges orchestral music and lives with his wife Christine in Massachusetts.